AF143848

BOOK ANALYSIS

By Tom O'Brien

The Sound and the Fury

BY WILLIAM FAULKNER

Bright
≡Summaries.com

WILLIAM FAULKNER 9

THE SOUND AND THE FURY 13

SUMMARY 17

April seventh 1928: Benjy
June second 1910: Quentin
April sixth 1928: Jason
April eighth 1928: Dilsey

CHARACTER STUDY 29

Benjy Compson
Caddy Compson
Quentin Compson (Caddy's brother)
Jason Compson IV
Dilsey Gibson
Caroline Compson
Jason Compson III
Quentin Compson (Caddy's daughter)

ANALYSIS 43

Origin of the title
Form and style
Southern society at the beginning of the 20th century

FURTHER REFLECTION 59

FURTHER READING 63

WILLIAM FAULKNER

AMERICAN NOVELIST AND SHORT STORY WRITER

- **Born in New Albany, Mississippi in 1897.**
- **Died in Byhalia, Mississippi in 1962.**
- **Notable works:**
  - *A Rose for Emily* (1930), short story
  - *As I Lay Dying* (1930), novel
  - *Absalom, Absalom!* (1936), novel

Born William Cuthbert Falkner (the correct spelling of his family name), the winner of the 1949 Nobel Prize in Literature grew up in a literary family while also learning to ride horses, hunt and fish. His strongest influences were his mother, who encouraged him to read and draw, and his nanny Caroline Barr.

He did not graduate from high school, and then managed to enlist in the Canadian Royal Airforce by pretending to be British, but World War I ended before he flew any active missions, which did not stop him from adopting the persona (and the uniform) of an RAF pilot when he returned to Mississippi.

Prior to 1926, when his debut novel *Soldiers' Pay* was published, he wrote mainly poetry and absorbed the work of modernists such as the British-American poet T.S. Elliot (1888-1965) and the Irish novelist James Joyce (1882-1941). He was advised by the American writer Sherwood Anderson (1876-1941) to write stories based on the rural Mississippi countryside that included his home town of Oxford, advice which resulted in his creation of the fictional Yoknapatawpha County, which became the setting for the majority of his novels.

When he published the controversial novel *Sanctuary* in 1931, it sold well and aroused interest in his earlier novels such as *The Sound and the Fury* (1929). This book, and his novels published during the 1930s, such as *Light in August* (1932) and *Absalom, Absalom!* (1936), are usually considered his best work, and have attracted more analyses and criticism than any other 20th century writer, due to his dense, challenging text full of symbolism, linguistic experimentation and deeply flawed characters.

Faulkner continued to write on difficult themes such as race, death and sexuality through the 1940s and 1950s. He died from thrombosis developed after a riding accident in 1962.

THE SOUND AND THE FURY

AN EXPERIMENTAL MODERNIST NOVEL

- **Genre:** modernist novel
- **Reference edition:** Faulkner, W. (1995) *The Sound and the Fury*. London: Vintage.
- **1st edition:** 1929
- **Themes:** the American South, childhood, family, race, sexuality

Faulkner began writing *The Sound and the Fury* during a lengthy period where he was unsuccessfully trying to get his previous novel published. Discouraged, but at the same time liberated, by the criticisms and rejections of agents and publishers, Faulkner wrote a novel that was highly experimental in its use of language and its non-linear narrative. It is now considered among the best American novels of the 20th century, and was certainly Faulkner's personal favourite among his 19 novels.

The first of the novel's four sections is written from the perspective of Benjy Compson, a severely mentally disabled man living with his aristocratic family and their black servants in rural Mississippi. The second and third sections are told from the perspectives of Benjy's two brothers: sensitive Quentin and vindictive Jason. The narratives of all three brothers range back and forth in time, and relate the gradual disintegration of the family, and the brothers' obsession with their sister Caddy.

The final section uses a more traditional narrative voice, and sets the dysfunction of the Compson family in stark contrast to the quiet dignity of their black housekeeper Dilsey Gibson.

SUMMARY

A note on Benjy's section: Faulkner originally intended this section to be printed in different coloured inks to make it easier for the reader to follow the timeline of events, which is disjointed and not presented chronologically. Only limited special editions have this feature. In most editions, italics are used to signify a switch in time. Since Benjy is unable to do anything except record what he sees and hears, many of the events concerning other people only become clear when reading the section narrated by Benjy's brother Jason.

APRIL SEVENTH 1928: BENJY

On his 33rd birthday, Benjy Compson follows his caretaker Luster around the Compson family estate in search of a coin that Luster has lost. They begin at the edge of the property where Benjy watches people play on the adjacent golf course. When the golfers call out to their caddies, reminding Benjy of his sister Caddy, it provokes a strong emotional response in him. As he and

Luster walk down to a stream and then return to the Compson house, various landmarks, smells and other stimulations set off memories that Benjy experiences as if for the first time.

Crawling through a fence takes Benjy back to 1902, when he and Caddy deliver a letter from their Uncle Maury to Mrs Patterson, a neighbour. The contents of the letter cause Mr Patterson to physically attack Maury, who swears revenge.

Passing the carriage house summons up a past carriage ride during which T. P., Luster's uncle, drives Benjy and his mother to the cemetery to visit the graves of Benjy's father and his brother Quentin. A teenage Jason refuses to accompany them, and complains about his Uncle Maury sponging money off his mother.

Visiting the stream provokes Benjy's memory of a day in 1898 when the four Compson children are sent away from the house with Versh, Luster's other uncle. The others refer to Benjy as Maury, the name he was given at birth. After playing in the stream, they return to the house, where Frony (who is a child in this scene, but becomes Luster's mother when she is older) blurts out her suspicion that the Compson children's grandmother has died. Caddy refuses to believe her and tries to spy through a window to prove Frony wrong, but the older Quentin suspects that Frony is telling the truth. The children are sent to bed in the house of Dilsey and Roskus (servants of the Compson family, and T. P., Versh and Frony's parents), still without being told of the death.

Passing the barn in his memory of 1898 causes Benjy's memory to jump forward to 1910, to the day of Caddy's wedding. T. P. steals alcohol from the cellar, gets drunk and also gives alcohol to Benjy. Quentin discovers them and beats T. P., but then gives Benjy more alcohol to keep him quiet.

When the children are sent to bed in Dilsey's house in 1898, this again causes another memory jump in Benjy, taking him to another time in the same house, when Roskus speaks of his belief in a curse on the Compson family, which is dismissed by Dilsey. This in turn sets off a series of other memories, in which Benjy hears Caddy and Dilsey discussing his name change from Maury to Benjamin, finds Caddy alone with a lover, witnesses the death of his father, plays with an infant Luster and Caddy's young daughter Quentin, and hears Roskus again speak of the curse.

Walking with Luster past the gate of the property sets off Benjy's memory of escaping and chasing some passing schoolgirls and then being dosed with an anaesthetic for an operation in which he is castrated.

Back in the present (April seventh 1928), Benjy eats birthday cake with Dilsey and Luster but then burns his hand on the stove. Dilsey opens the stove so Benjy can watch the fire, which calms him but sets off another sequence of memories, in which Benjy visits his mother in her sickroom, witnesses a fight between Caddy and Jason, and relives his pain as Caddy is banished from the house by their mother.

Later, Benjy finds Caddy's daughter Quentin in a similar situation – alone with a lover in a secluded part of the property – to the one in which he found her mother several years earlier. Benjy then witnesses a furious row between Quentin and his brother Jason – now head of the household – about her behaviour.

JUNE SECOND 1910: QUENTIN

Benjy's brother Quentin wakes up in his room at Harvard University, and is bothered by the sound of his watch, which he inherited from his grandfather. He returns to bed, recalling in turn his father giving him the watch and the painful memory of Caddy's wedding announcement. His roommate Shreve tells him he will be late for class if he does not leave soon. As he watches Shreve head to his first class from the window, Quentin recalls falsely confessing to his father that he had committed incest with his sister Caddy and his father's refusal to believe the story. He returns to his room and destroys the face and hands of his watch, before heading to the post office to mail a letter to his father, and then going for breakfast.

Quentin then visits a shop to enquire about having his watch repaired, and then another to buy two heavy weights. He catches a train with no clear destination in mind, and gets off the train near a bridge over the Charles River (Cambridge, Massachusetts). At the bridge he watches Gerald Bland, a fellow student, set off in a rowing boat, and again thinks about his sister Caddy and his resentment of her promiscuous behaviour. He also seems to be contemplating his own suicide by drowning. He runs into Deacon, a black man who works running errands for students at the university, and gives him a letter for his room-mate Shreve.

He then catches a trolley (tram) and again sinks into memories of Caddy, recalling how he confronted her fiancé Herbert Head before the wedding and then attempted to convince Caddy, who was not sure who the father of her unborn child is, to run away with him instead of going ahead with the wedding.

Later, Quentin buys food for a hungry Italian girl at a bakery, who then starts to follow him. He searches for her home, but is then arrested when the girl's brother accuses him of kidnapping. He negotiates his release and joins Shreve, Gerald Bland, a fellow student called Spoade, two young women and Bland's mother, who are on their way to a picnic. Recalling a fight between himself and Dalton Ames, who may be the father of Caddy's unborn child, Quentin picks a fight with Gerald Bland, who Quentin feels treats women in a similar fashion to Ames. Quentin ends up badly beaten.

Quentin then returns to Harvard, where he tidies his things, dresses neatly and prepares to leave. It is now clear that he is going to go through with his plan to kill himself, and that the letters to his father and Shreve are suicide notes.

APRIL SIXTH 1928: JASON

On the morning of the day before Benjy's narration, his brother Jason confronts his mother Caroline about the behaviour of his niece Quentin, who frequently skips school and whom they suspect has had multiple relationships with men. Jason threatens to take over the job of keeping Quentin under control, and attempts to beat her at breakfast, but is prevented from doing so by Dilsey and Caroline. He then drives Quentin to school and arrives late to his job at the local store in Jefferson.

A short time later Jason collects his mail from the post office, which includes a letter from his mistress in Memphis and a cheque from his banished sister Caddy, intended for her daughter's expenses. The letter sparks a series of memories, including the funeral of his father, the elder Jason Compson, which Caddy, having already been thrown out by her husband Herbert Head and banished from the Compson family home, attends in secret. She begs her brother to allow her to see her daughter, which he agrees to do in return for money. Jason then recalls his efforts to prevent Caddy from having any access to her daughter, which include threats to have Dilsey Gibson fired and Benjy sent to an institution.

It becomes clear that Jason considers himself the sole breadwinner of the family, and unfairly cheated out of the lucrative job offered to him by Caddy's husband, which makes it easy for him to justify to himself his theft of the money that Caddy sends her daughter. The method of his fraud is revealed as he searches for a fake cheque to give to his mother – who has the habit of burning the checks sent by Caddy – and describes how he has power of attorney over his mother's affairs. He uses some of the extra funds to invest in the stock market, and blames his poor performance on a belief in a Jewish conspiracy to defraud investors. He even manages to take most of a money order that Caddy has sent to her daughter directly.

He later observes Quentin pass the store in the company of a performer from the travelling show which is in town for the weekend. Infuriated by this, he follows them on foot and then by car, but they evade his pursuit. Jason is heavily sarcastic towards his boss at the store who dares to criticise him for not attending to his work. At supper later that night, Jason takes out some of his rage on Dilsey and Luster, before having a furious argument with Quentin, who clearly suspects him of stealing her money. After Quentin storms out, Jason even resorts to bullying his mother, who considers him her only normal child and is mostly blind to his faults.

APRIL EIGHTH 1928: DILSEY

On the morning of Easter Sunday, Dilsey Gibson emerges from her tiny shack and heads to the kitchen of the Compson house to prepare breakfast. Realising that her grandson Luster is sleeping late after attending the show the previous night, she has to light the fire herself, as well as prepare the meal. She struggles to do this and attend to Caroline's petty requests at the same time. Jason then forces her to fetch Quentin for breakfast, but they soon realise that Quentin's room is empty. Caroline jumps to the conclusion that Quentin has committed suicide like her namesake, but Jason realises the truth: that Quentin has discovered where he keeps the money he has stolen from her, and escaped.

As Jason storms off to hunt for Quentin, Dilsey gets ready to attend the Easter service at the local church, and decides to take Benjy with her instead of leaving him with the hysterical Caroline. She walks to the Church with Benjy, her daughter Frony and grandson Luster through the town of Jefferson, and is greeted with respect and reverence by the other black residents. At the church, a guest preacher begins his service speaking in a polished, educated manner. When he switches to a more emotional way of preaching, speaking in the black southern dialect, his service has a deep effect on both Dilsey, who weeps openly, and Benjy, whose usual agitation is soothed. Back at home, Dilsey and Luster are unable to keep Benjy quiet, so Dilsey tells Luster to drive Benjy in the carriage to visit the graveyard where his father and brother are buried.

As Dilsey is attending the church service, Jason drives to the sheriff's office in Jefferson and demands that the sheriff help him to track down Quentin. The sheriff refuses to help Jason, citing the lack of evidence, but really acting out of a strong dislike of Jason and a suspicion of his financial dealings. Jason decides to act alone, and drives to the next town, hoping that Quentin and her lover travelled there with the other performers from the show. Jason fails to find them there, and is in such a terrible physical state that he has to pay a local man to drive him back to Jefferson.

Luster drives Benjy towards the graveyard, but drives around the town square in the opposite direction to which Benjy is accustomed. This causes Benjy extreme distress, and Jason –who is recovering in his car parked on the square – throws Luster violently from the carriage and reverses its direction. Benjy stops screaming and relaxes as the trip resumes its familiar order.

CHARACTER STUDY

Note on the characters' physical appearance:
As the first three sections of the novel are told by the three Compson brothers, the principal characters (the Compson and Gibson families) are not physically described; Benjy is unable to, and Quentin and Jason have no need to describe the people they know so well (though Quentin's fellow Harvard students are described in detail). We have to wait until the final section with its omniscient narrator before we learn of some characters' appearances. Consequently, characters who are not present for the events of April eighth 1928 (the elder Jason Compson, and his son and daughter Quentin and Caddy) are never really described physically.

BENJY COMPSON

Benjy is the severely mentally disabled son of Jason and Caroline Compson. Named after his uncle Maury at birth, his mother insists on changing his name when she becomes aware of the extent of his disability, which she does not want associated with her side of the family. As an adult, he is a large man, lacking any body hair due to his castration as a teenager, who has "a shambling gait like a trained bear" (p. 274) and eyes "the pale, sweet blue of cornflowers" (*ibid*.). He is unable to speak or interpret events, and does not differentiate between past and present events. As a result, the section of the novel 'narrated' by Benjy reads as a series of visual impressions and any dialogue within his hearing, as if Benjy is simply an audio and video recorder.

Benjy does not change or develop over the course of time, and therefore plays (as far he is able to) with the different generations of children in the novel in exactly the same way. The only time he shows a sign of physical development, becoming aroused and chasing local schoolgirls when the gate to the property is left open, is brutally halted by his castration.

Of his three siblings, Quentin seems mostly indifferent to Benjy, being completely wrapped up in his own concerns and his obsession with Caddy. Jason sees Benjy as an affliction on the family, pushes for his institutionalisation, and may have had much more to do with Benjy's castration than he admits. Caddy is the only member of Benjy's own family to show him true affection. She therefore unintentionally divides Benjy's otherwise 'timeless' existence into two parts: his life with her, and his life without her after her banishment, during which he seeks out and is temporarily comforted by things that remind him of her.

Benjy's memories of childhood (1898 and 1902) show a time when the Compsons were a more cohesive unit and at least took responsibility for his care. By the time of his later memories, the family has started to come apart, and Benjy is taken care of almost entirely by Dilsey and her sons and grandson, who are much more skilled than any Compson (besides Caddy) at understanding his needs.

CADDY COMPSON

Caddy (Candace) Compson is the second-oldest child of Jason and Caroline. She is the happiest and best-adjusted of the siblings until she reaches adolescence, when her burgeoning sexuality leads to multiple affairs, then later her pregnancy, failed marriage and banishment from the family home. She is forced to leave her daughter Quentin in the care of her parents and Dilsey.

Although she is the only one of the four Compson children not to narrate a section of the novel, Caddy, her actions, and then her absence are central to the plot. This centrality arises largely from her three brothers' preoccupation with her and her behaviour:

- Benjy's repetition of "Caddy smelled like trees" (p. 40) is the most powerful suggestion that he is not just a 'dumb witness' to the events in the novel, but also possesses an inner emotional life, largely thanks to his sister. When Caddy wears perfume, it is as if she does not exist for Benjy.
- Quentin's obsession with his sister's sexuality, and inability to come to terms with it, is summed up in the passage "Why don't you bring him into the house, Caddy? Why must you do like nigger women do in the pasture the ditches the dark woods hot hidden furious in the dark woods" (p. 90).
- Jason displays his almost sociopathic vindictiveness, selfishness and lack of empathy

when he (at both the beginning and end of his section) brutally dismisses Caddy's life with "once a bitch always a bitch" (p. 179, p. 264).

The importance of the character of Caddy is not found in her actions, but in her family's reaction to her perfectly normal and natural behaviour. The central tragedy of the novel is that Quentin, Jason and their mother's refusal to accept Caddy for who she is separates her from Benjy, and ends the only truly loving and nourishing relationship within the family.

QUENTIN COMPSON (CADDY'S BROTHER)

Quentin is the oldest of the four Compson children. He is sent to Harvard University using funds from the sale of part of the family estate. He is emotionally sensitive, and ill-equipped to deal with the realities of life, both at home and in Massachusetts.

The announcement of Caddy's marriage to Herbert Head sends him into a spiral of depression that he is unable to recover from. His depression is characterised by intense reflection on his father's cynical and fatalistic view of life, and painful memories revolving around his 'loss' of his sister Caddy when she becomes sexually active, in contrast to his own continued virginity.

There are some remarkable similarities between Quentin Compson and Holden Caulfield, the narrator and protagonist of *The Catcher in the Rye* (1951) by J. D. Salinger (American writer, 1919-2010). Both are depressed, and both have the misguided sense that they are responsible for protecting their sisters' innocence (Holden is destined to fail at this impossible task in which Quentin has already failed), and both get into fights because of a fellow student's perceived lack of respect for women (both lose badly). Quentin's aimless journey along the Charles River is also mirrored by Holden's trip to New York.

Due to his fixation on his father and sister, Quentin's feelings about the other members of his family are not clear. Likewise, Quentin's character is largely confined to his own section, and his family members' feelings about his suicide remain unclear; Benjy does not feel his absence as he does Caddy's, and Jason hardly mentions his older brother.

JASON COMPSON IV

Jason Compson is Jason Sr. and Caroline's third-oldest child. As an adult, he appears "cold and shrewd, with close-thatched brown hair [...] like a caricature of a bartender" (p. 279). He shows early evidence of his vindictiveness when he destroys some paper dolls that Caddy had made for Benjy (p. 63). By the time of his adulthood in the novel's 'present' (April 1928), he has developed into something of a monster. His life is dominated by two major obsessions: money, and his hatred of his absent sister Caddy and her daughter Quentin.

Though some of his resentments have a basis in reality (he did not receive the expensive schooling of his older brother and sister due to the family's diminished financial circumstances, and the income from his job is necessary for the household), he also uses imaginary or exaggerated grievances to justify his behaviour, especially his theft of the money Caddy regularly sends for her daughter's expenses.

He is the most overtly racist of the Compsons, referring to Dilsey Gibson and her family as a "kitchenful of niggers" (p. 278), and making constant references to the supposed laziness and untrustworthiness of black people in general, and Dilsey's family in particular.

Despite being by far the most unpleasant character in the novel, Jason is adept at seeing the other characters' real faults along with those he imagines. He also provides the clearest picture of some of the key events of the novel, and is often the considered the funniest character in all of Faulkner's novels.

DILSEY GIBSON

Dilsey Gibson is the Compson family's housekeeper and nanny to the children. She is a big, strong woman, though diminished in stature by the time of the novel's present, with "a collapsed face that gave the impression of the bones themselves being outside the skin" (p. 266). The last section of the novel reveals her intense religious faith. She provides strong discipline to her own children, the Compson children and to her grandson Luster, while also showing great kindness and patience toward them, especially Benjy.

In the earlier parts of the novel, when her husband Roskus and the elder Jason Compson are still alive, Dilsey defers to them as heads of their respective households, but with their deaths, she becomes the most naturally authoritative person on the Compson property. Though she must remain obedient to direct commands from Caroline and the younger Jason, she effectively manages Caroline's sometimes ridiculous demands, and she is especially resistant to Jason's tyranny, even physically defending Quentin (Caddy's daughter) against a beating (p. 184).

The rest of Dilsey's family are as follows:

- **Roskus:** Dilsey's husband. Poor health is already preventing him from working around the time of the elder Jason's Compson's death. He is highly superstitious, and believes that Benjy's disability and Quentin's suicide are evidence of a curse on the Compsons.
- **Versh:** Dilsey's eldest son. He takes on the role of Benjy's caretaker during Benjy's childhood, and later leaves the Compson estate to find work.
- **Frony:** Dilsey's daughter. She lives on the estate but does not seem to work directly

serving the Compsons. As a child she plays with the Compsons and informs them of their grandmother's death when Caroline and the elder Jason try to keep it from them.

- **T. P.:** Dilsey's younger son. T. P. becomes Benjy's caretaker after Versh. He gets drunk during Caddy's wedding and is attacked by Quentin.
- **Luster:** Dilsey's grandson. He has become Benjy's main caretaker by the time of the novel's present. He is less obedient than his two uncles, and sometimes teases and bullies Benjy out of boredom.

CAROLINE COMPSON

Caroline Compson is the mother of Quentin, Caddy, Jason and Benjy. In April 1928, she appears "cold and querulous, with perfect white hair and eyes pouched and baffled and so dark as to appear to be all pupil" (p. 279). She is a hypochondriac, constantly complaining of feeling unwell and staying in bed for long periods. She is highly conscious of the lower social status of her side of the family (the Bascombs) compared to her husband's illustrious family name. She seeks to balance this by ascribing the faults of her children – Caddy's promiscuity, Benjy's disability and Quentin's suicide – to the Compson bloodline, and ignoring the faults of her brother Maury and son Jason, whom she considers a Bascomb.

At one point in Quentin's section of the novel, he laments that "if I'd just had a mother so I could say Mother Mother" (p. 171). Despite Quentin's self-pitying attitude, he provides an insight into the attitude of Caroline towards her children. She feels that, as teenagers, Quentin and Caddy "were always conspiring against me" (p. 261). She also has little patience for Benjy, never learning the 'art' of calming him down that Caddy and the Gibson family become adept at. She even alienates Jason, her favourite, by making him the chief target of her complaints and insecurities after Caddy's banishment and the deaths of Quentin and his father.

By refusing to accept any responsibility for the tragic outcomes of her children's lives, Caroline makes herself an object of pity and disgust for all the Compsons and Gibsons who remain at the estate in 1928.

JASON COMPSON III

Jason Compson III is the father of Quentin, Caddy, Jason and Benjy. Like his wife, but to a slightly lesser extent, he is guilty of distant and neglectful parenting. He is full of pride, and does nothing to ease his wife's insecurities about their relative social status, treating her brother with amusement and disdain.

Although Quentin may be an unreliable narrator and his accounts of conversations with his father may therefore be somewhat inaccurate, it seems that his father was uncaring, even to the extent of mocking the obsessions and insecurities of his eldest son. According to Quentin, his father passed on his own father's watch to Quentin with the words "I give you the mausoleum of all hope and desire" (p. 73). This nihilistic attitude, an insistence that nothing really matters and that hope is pointless, has a powerful effect on Quentin and perhaps contributes to his suicide.

However, there also appears to be another side to the elder Jason's character. He shows some affection towards Caddy and Benjy as children, and also a desire to keep the family together, appearing to disagree with Caddy's banishment and the idea of sending Benjy to an institution. However, his death due to alcoholism leaves Caddy, her daughter Quentin, Benjy and the Gibson family exposed to the whims of Caroline and the younger Jason.

QUENTIN COMPSON (CADDY'S DAUGHTER)

Quentin Compson, born and named shortly after her uncle's suicide, is the daughter of Caddy and an unknown father. She is strong-willed and rebellious, and her adolescence mirrors that of her mother's. She hates her uncle Jason with a passion and, as she gets older, becomes fully aware of his scheme to defraud her. Away from her mother's influence, she fails to develop any empathy for Benjy, and the idea of sending him away to an institution is the only thing that she and Jason agree upon. She shows courage and initiative in taking the money that Jason has stolen from her over the years, and escaping.

ANALYSIS

ORIGIN OF THE TITLE

The title of the novel comes from one of the speeches by the titular character of William Shakespeare's (English playwright, 1564-1616) play *Macbeth* (1623):

> "Tomorrow, and tomorrow, and tomorrow
> Creeps in this petty pace from day to day,
> To the last syllable of recorded time,
> And all our yesterdays have lighted fools
> The way to dusty death. Out, out, brief candle!
> Life's but a walking shadow, a poor player
> That struts and frets his hour upon the stage
> And then is heard no more. It is a tale
> Told by an idiot, full of sound and fury
> Signifying nothing." (*Macbeth*, V.v.19–28)

The connection between 'a tale told by an idiot' and Benjy's section is obvious, and the novel's last act is 'full of sound and fury' as Benjy's distress reaches a peak when Luster drives him the wrong way round the town square. It is also possible to hunt for other connections, such as the possibility that Quentin is attempting to stop the 'petty pace' from creeping in as he ignores his roommate's warning to hurry to class and then breaks his grandfather's watch. His brother Jason is most certainly 'a poor actor who struts'. Finally, it is not known whether or not Faulkner considered that his favourite of all his novels signified nothing, but *The Sound and the Fury* is certainly one of the reasons why he is still being heard quite some time after his 'hour upon the stage' ended.

FORM AND STYLE

Faulkner often claimed to be a 'farmer', to have a limited formal education and few interests outside of rural Mississippi, which he inhabited for most of his life. The subject matter of his work, including *The Sound and the Fury*, would seem to reinforce this idea, but the reality was quite different. By the early 1920s, Faulkner was fully engaged with both contemporary literary trends and current affairs.

One key aspect of this engagement was the rise of modernist literature and poetry, which led writers and poets to consciously try to break with traditional forms of poetry and narrative and experiment with new forms and styles of writing. This experimentation included the development of 'stream of consciousness' writing, in which the writer attempts to record the subjective, internal experience of a character, rather than telling the story through an omniscient narrator. Although his previous novel *Flags in the Dust* (first published as *Sartoris* in 1929) lacked many characteristics of traditional narrative fiction, *The Sound and the Fury* began as Faulkner's first true experiment with literary modernism and stream of consciousness writing.

As a result of the experimental nature of the work, readers often find Benjy and Quentin's sections extremely challenging to read, but then feel rewarded by the frenetic pace of the action and the humour in Jason's section, and also by the rich descriptive writing as they are lifted out of the Compson brothers' perspectives in the final section.

Faulkner scholars Noel Polk and Theresa M. Towner provide some excellent insights into how Faulkner's modernist experiments with language and structure helped him to represent the inner lives of the Compson brothers, while allowing the tragic story of the Compsons to slowly emerge. These insights will be explored in the following sections.

Benjy

Towner writes of *The Sound and the Fury* that "its structure, like its title, invites us to participate in solving a mystery" (Towner, 2008: 148). She is referring to the disjointed chronology of the novel as a whole, and within Benjy's section in particular. Benjy cannot differentiate between the past and the present, so the reader has to hunt for clues to gain some idea of what has happened to the Compsons, and in what order, between 1898 and 1928. Even then, they will have to wait for Jason's section for confirmation and clarification of some of the events.

In Benjy's section, the language as well as the structure provides mysteries that the reader can solve. On the very first page, Benjy sees red and yellow flags and repeats the observation "they were hitting" (p. 1) several times. That Benjy is watching people play golf is something that readers have to work out for themselves. In using language in this way, Faulkner is also inviting the reader to assess the extent of Benjy's disability. In failing to say 'they were playing golf', Benjy shows that his ability to grasp concepts is well below that of even very young children, and when he tells us 'they were hitting little' (either they were hitting gently, as in putting, or that they were playing on a part of the course further away), we learn that "he experiences the world as a jumbled and unstable convergence of un-connected phenomena" (Polk, 1993: 141).

Rereading Benjy's section after finishing the novel, without some of the frustration that is common on the first attempt, can lead to a greater appreciation of Faulkner's daring and innovative use of language to represent the inner life of a neurologically impaired individual (nearly three-quarters of a century before Mark Haddon's [English novelist, born in 1962] *The Curious Incident of the Dog in the Night-Time* was published in 2003).

Quentin

In some ways, Quentin's narrative provides the reader with a much clearer picture of events than Benjy's. Quentin differentiates more clearly between the past and the present, offers detailed descriptions of other characters and his own insights into their behaviour, and provides a much wider physical perspective as he wanders through the surroundings of Harvard on his final day of life. However, when the past does intrude into his thoughts, his narrative becomes even more confused and difficult to follow than Benjy's.

Polk explains this difference by proposing that Faulkner used variation in language to represent Quentin's lapses into memories that are extremely painful and confusing:

> "One can trace Quentin's psychic disintegration, his movements into and out of lucidity, in the degree of normality of his language's representation, from the intricately structured sentences of some passages, to the almost complete disintegration of traditional language representation in others." (Polk, 1993: 150)

With this in mind, Quentin's straightforward narration of his actions on the final page of his section (p. 178) takes on a very chilling quality, as it suggests that he is much more at peace as heads out to throw himself into a river than he would be to continue tormenting himself with memories of his father and sister.

Jason

The more straightforward language of Jason's section shows that he has the adult sense of himself that Benjy lacks, but does not have the same advanced intellectual curiosity as Quentin. The replacement of 'said' with 'says' in his narrative shows that he lives much more in the present moment than his brothers. He has an ego which his brothers lack (Benjy due to his disability, Quentin because of his crushing depression), which allows him to remain in control of his narrative.

Although Jason provides clarity, and clears up many of the events that remain uncertain in Benjy and Quentin's sections, his excessive self-regard and his prejudices make him a less reliable narrator than his brothers; Benjy lacks the ability to omit things that he witnesses or embellish facts, and Quentin, at what he knows to be the end of his life, has no reason for dishonesty. Faulkner represents Jason's unreliability by having him use

'I says' in his inner thoughts for witty and cutting remarks which he does not actually say out loud. Towner writes that "[Jason's] insistence on rhetorical power masks a fragile ego" (Towner, 2008: 22) and that his character has a "psychic depth", in that he hides things from himself, and therefore the reader, whereas his brothers do not (Towner, 2008: 21). Polk agrees, writing that Jason "keeps himself talking loudly so that he won't have to listen to the voices that threaten him: he drowns out one horrendous noise with an even more horrendous one" (Polk, 1993: 156).

SOUTHERN SOCIETY AT THE BEGINNING OF THE 20TH CENTURY

Aristocracy

The idea of a Southern 'aristocracy' developed as early landowners in the British colonies of Virginia and the Carolinas employed, first, indentured servants arriving from Europe and, second, African slaves as the Atlantic slave trade flourished in the 16th, 17th and 18th centuries. This pattern persisted as the colonies became the United States and allowed certain landowners to increase their holdings into huge plantations, and to cultivate a leisurely lifestyle in which they enjoyed some of the same luxuries as their European counterparts. This form of society spread westwards where the lifestyle of Virginian and Carolinian plantation owners was imitated by large landowners in newer states such as Faulkner's Mississippi. Even after the conflict between the agrarian, slave-holding states of the Southern US against the industrialising, non-slave states of the North escalated into the American Civil War (1861-1865), the governments imposed on the Southern states by the US federal government (known as Reconstruction governments) failed to implement land reforms, and some plantation-owning families were able to maintain their aristocratic lifestyles, or at least the illusion of them, into the 20th century.

The Compson family in *The Sound and the Fury* represents the persistence of a form of society that was fast becoming obsolete in the face of late 19th and early 20th-century economic developments (represented in the novel by the sale of most of their remaining productive land, which is turned into a golf course). The elder Jason

Compson appears to live by the ideals and myths of the Southern aristocracy as he, his wife and her brother Maury have all their needs (cooking, running the estate, and the vast majority of childcare) met by a black family living on their estate. Jason seems to take care to instil these values in his eldest son Quentin, who commits suicide when his sister fails to live up to the myth of the Southern 'lady'. The younger Jason Compson abandons this way of life in favour of the single-minded pursuit of money, and is unconcerned about appearing to be a 'gentle-man', even though he is quite happy to use his position as head of the family to advance his own interests.

Race

Just as with land reform, the Reconstruction governments mostly failed in their attempts to enforce racial equality and the rights of new black citizens, especially in 'Deep South' states such as Mississippi. In *The Sound and the Fury*, Dilsey and her husband Roskus are old enough to have been born into slavery (before 1865), and they and their family's lives reflect how former slaves' circumstances both changed and stayed the same following the abolition of slavery. By 1928, two of their sons (Versh and T. P.) have left to find work, and Dilsey demonstrates that she has her own sources of income when she pays for Benjy's 33rd birthday cake (p. 57). She also has no hesitation in standing up for others against Jason's bullying. However, she is unable to refuse a direct command from either Jason or his mother, and her family apparently has no choice in the matter of taking care of Benjy when the remaining Compsons refuse to either send him to an institution or to take care of him themselves. The persistence of Southern 'aristocratic' values into the 20th century was accompanied by the insistence of the majority of white Southerners that black people were only fit to be employed as domestic servants, or to become tenant farmers with white landowners; independent landowning or working in a profession was to remain the exception rather than the rule for black people in the South for many years yet. This was backed up by an implicit threat of violence.

Two different forms of racial prejudice are shown by the brothers Jason and Quentin during their sections of the novel. When his train stops, Quentin throws a coin to a black man waiting at the crossing and tells him to "buy yourself some santy claus" (p. 85). This patronising, paternalistic kind of racism is another holdover from the 19th-century plantation way of life, passed on to Quentin through his father. Jason on the other hand, displays a much more violent and virulent racism, constantly referring to the supposed shortcomings of the 'niggers' who work from him and his colleague at the store. As Jason does not share his brother and father's values, he instead embodies the bolder, nastier racism that was a product of the backlash against demands for freedom and equality, and led to the restriction of voting rights for black Southerners, segregation and the frequent lynchings that aimed to instil fear into black Southerners who tried to assert their rights, get an education or advance themselves economically.

Faulkner shows his keen awareness of the reality of living as a black American in the 20th century through Quentin's description of his relationship with Deacon, a black man who makes a living doing errands for Harvard students like Quentin.

Quentin describes the process by which Deacon takes on a different persona depending on which white people he is talking to. Richard Wright, a black American author (1908-1960), confirms the validity of this brief observation of Faulkner's in much greater detail in his novel *Native Son* (1940) and autobiography *Black Boy* (1945). Demonstrating a sophisticated understanding of race relations (much more acute than many contemporary professional historians) without making any overt political statements on their injustice is a common feature of Faulkner's work.

Sexuality

Faulkner claimed that the image of a girl with muddy underwear was his starting point in writing *The Sound and the Fury*. This image, occurring when Caddie climbs a tree to see into the window of the house (p. 37), cannot possibly have a sexual meaning for Benjy, but perhaps marks the beginning of the slightly older Quentin's awareness of his and his sister's sexual difference. The image takes on great significance in the light of Caddy's future sexual 'transgressions' (in the eyes of her mother, husband and brothers).

Though Caddy's sexuality causes her a certain amount of shame and regret, these feelings arise from her witnessing the pain of her brothers Quentin, who feels he has failed to protect her innocence, and Benjy, who cannot possibly understand why she has to leave (she also regrets the power over her life that her past behaviour appears to give her brother Jason). She does not, however, regret the acts themselves, showing a refusal to internalise the attitudes towards sex and sexuality shown by her family. Faulkner, according to Towner, shows a strong "sympathy with objects of sexual desire" (Towner, 2008: p. 87) in much of his work. The blame for Caddy's enforced separation from the family does not lie with Caddy herself, but with her mother, who embodies a certain societal attitude toward female sexuality which is also responsible for Quentin's emotional torment and eventual suicide.

FURTHER REFLECTION

SOME QUESTIONS TO THINK ABOUT...

- Why do you think Faulkner opens the novel with Benjy's section, set on April seventh, rather than Jason's, which is set on April sixth?
- Why does Quentin only send suicide notes to his father and his roommate?
- What is the significance of the church service in the final section? Why does the preacher shift from standard speech to the black Southern vernacular during his sermon?
- Why do you think Dilsey stays with the Compsons in the face of Caroline and Jason's demands and abuse?
- Why do you think Frony, Dilsey's daughter, is not involved in serving the Compsons or looking after Benjy?
- Faulkner describes in detail the relationships between the white aristocratic Compson family and their black servants, without ever referring explicitly to the wider political and

social context of Southern race relations. Do you think this means that Faulkner was unconcerned about the political and social status of black Southerners?

- In the novel's final act, Jason rushes to correct Luster's mistake and to calm Benjy. Is this a sign that Jason is truly attached to his brother, or does he just want him to stop screaming in public?
- Many of Faulkner's characters, including Quentin (brother) find the smell of flowers oppressive and unpleasant. Why do you think this is?

We want to hear from you!
Leave a comment on your online library
and share your favourite books on social media!

FURTHER READING

REFERENCE EDITION

- Faulkner, W. (1995) *The Sound and the Fury*. London: Vintage.

REFERENCE STUDIES

- Polk, N. (1993) Trying Not to Say: A Primer on the Language of *The Sound and the Fury*. In: Polk, N. ed. (1993) *New Essays on* The Sound and the Fury. Cambridge: Cambridge University Press, pp. 139-175. [Online]. [Accessed 15 November 2018]. Available from: <https://doi.org/10.1017/CBO9780511620485>

- Shakespeare, W. (1993) *Macbeth*. New York: Dover Publications.

- Towner, T. (2008). *The Cambridge Introduction to William Faulkner*. Cambridge: Cambridge University Press. [Online]. [Accessed 15 November 2018]. Available from: <https://doi.org/10.1017/CBO9780511817045>

ADDITIONAL SOURCES

- Faulkner, W. (1949) *Nobel Prize acceptance speech*. [Online]. [Accessed 15 November 2018]. Available from: <https://www.nobelprize.org/prizes/literature/1949/faulkner/speech>

- Lewis, P. (2007). *The Cambridge Introduction to Modernism*. Cambridge: Cambridge University Press. [Online]. [Accessed 15 November 2018]. Available from: <https://doi.org/10.1017/CBO9780511803055>

MORE FROM BRIGHTSUMMARIES.COM

- Reading guide – *The Wishing Tree* by William Faulkner.

Although the editor makes every effort to
verify the accuracy of the information published,
BrightSummaries.com accepts no responsibility for
the content of this book.

www.brightsummaries.com

Ebook EAN: 9782808015479

Paperback EAN: 9782808015486

Legal Deposit: D/2018/12603/532

Cover: © Primento

Digital conception by Primento, the digital partner of
publishers.